You Rock!

CRUSH
AND
DOMINATE

13 STRATEGIES TO PISS OFF YOUR COMPETITORS

ERIK SWANSON

Habitude Warrior International

Published by Habitude Warrior International
in association with
Elite Online Publishing
ISBN: 978-1-5451-3864-9

This book is dedicated to all of those people who I have come across in my life who didn't believe in me... who said that I couldn't do it... to those who didn't put faith in me or lend me their support when I asked for it, or even begged for it. It may sound ruthless, but I thank you for showing me your true colors and allowing me to excel past you with flying colors!

Thank you!

Erik "Mr. Awesome" Swanson

"*Your thoughts determine your attitude. Your attitude determines your habits. Your 'HABITUDES' determine your future!*"

-Erik Swanson

PREFACE

INTRODUCTION: No More Games! That's right! No more games! I'd like to warn you, the reader, that this book you hold in your hands is not for the faint of heart. It's not for those who feel that we should all hold hands and sing together from the top of a mountain. This book is for those who realize that no matter what people seem to think, there will always be competitors out there in each of our industries. There is always going to be someone out there who secretly wants you to fail so that they can succeed. Sounds harsh, doesn't it? Well, the truth is sometimes eye-opening. I'm here to help you open your eyes and give you step-by-step strategies to crush your competitors! In the chapters that follow, we will explore the mental game of your competition, the techniques to use to beat them at this game and also to beat them to the punch! I want to be very clear that this book is NOT for everyone! In fact, I may even upset a few readers. But, please understand that this is simply a blueprint for you if you are frustrated with others passing you by in your industry. Take these steps and build your empire while dominating and crushing your competitors!

TABLE OF CONTENTS

"IF YOU ARE NOT WILLING
TO RISK THE UNUSUAL,
YOU WILL HAVE TO SETTLE
FOR THE ORDINARY."
-JIM ROHN

TIMES ARE TOUGH

Look around you. How many competitors do you have in your industry in the same city or area you work in? Seriously, take a good, long, hard look at it. I bet you would agree that there are way too many people in your same industry, with similar products or services, doing the same things and prospecting the same exact people you are trying to prospect.

Aren't you getting kind of sick of hearing your prospects telling you that they have already been approached by your competitors? Or, they tell you that they are all set because they already have a current provider for what you are offering.

Times are tough, and it's about time for us to buckle down and get really good at what we do so that we can convert more prospects into long-lasting clients. But, the serious truth is that we also need to realize that this game of success may require us to get a little dirty sometimes.

"It Doesn't Matter Where
You Came From.
All That Matters
Is Where You Are Going."
-Brian Tracy

THE MENTAL GAME

Make no mistake about it; there is an inner mental game that is played every time in every industry in any market across the planet. This mental game sometimes gets the best of us and allows others to pass us by on the success highway. Enough is enough. It's time for us to harness our mental game to allow our success to shine through.

There are two sides to the 'mental game.' The first side is *your* inner thoughts. The second side is your *competitor's* inner thoughts. The goal is to make sure you are in charge of *both,* and your success is inevitable.

What do I mean by being in charge of both? Well, we will work on ours first. But by the time you have mastered all of the following strategies, you will actually be in charge of your competitor's mindset and inner thoughts without even realizing it. It's a fantastic thing of beauty!

"YOU WILL GET ALL YOU WANT IN LIFE,
IF YOU HELP ENOUGH OTHER PEOPLE
GET WHAT THEY WANT."
-ZIG ZIGLAR

Your Inner Game

Your attitude will absolutely determine your altitude. This famous saying has been repeated time and time again… and it's so true! If you believe you can succeed and also crush your competitors at the same time, then it shall be. There is something about parts of our brains that want to be in harmony with each other. I'm speaking about our subconscious minds as well as our conscious minds. Whatever you tell your sub-conscious mind, it accepts as a 'command' and tries everything to adhere to that command. So, if you constantly tell yourself (and your sub-conscious mind) that you are GREAT, then your brain goes to work and looks for reasons to support you in that command. You start remembering experiences in your life in which you were great. You start 'convincing' yourself this is actually true, and your conscious mind will start taking the reins to match your sub-conscious mind. What's really awesome about this is that your subconscious mind doesn't know the difference between what is real or what is made up. Think of what you were dreaming, and you wake up in a major sweat and thought it was completely real. That's your sub-conscious mind at work.

So, the trick for you to learn is to constantly tell yourself that you are the envy of your competition. Repeat to yourself on a daily, even hourly basis, that *YOU ARE THE BEST!* Commands like these will seep into your mind and become a natural thought for you. This is what you want! Here is a Creed that I say to myself each and every day that hangs in my office. I even hang this on my mirror, so I see it every morning when I wake up to go brush my teeth and get my day started.

"THE STARTING POINT OF ALL
ACHIEVEMENT IS DESIRE."
-NAPOLEON HILL

COMPETITOR'S INNER GAME

One of the master techniques you will learn in this book is how to control your competitor's inner game made up of two components. Here's how it works.

The Two Components:

Your competitor's inner game is made up of two components.

#1 By controlling *your* daily inner game and thought patterns.

#2 By being a visible marketing threat to your competitor's production.

The more visible you and your company are in the eyes of your competition the more this will lower their positive attitude, and their inner game will suffer. It sounds harsh, but our goal here is to keep growing our positive attitude for ourselves as well as our team members in our company, while at the same time affecting your competition to get as frustrated as possible. This will decrease their production!

TIME TO GET DIRTY

Don't get me wrong. I'm not saying that we are going to do anything unethical! No, that's definitely not what I'm saying. And, as many of you know me, my style, and my philosophies, I'm a firm believer in the concept of 'Collaboration vs. Competition'. But, at the same time, wouldn't you agree that you do not want to collaborate with *ALL* of your competition? There comes a time and place for us to put our foot down and draw a line in the sand. It's time for us to learn the secrets and strategies of high achievers and top producers to beat out our competition and *get the sale!* In the following chapters, I will share with you 10 of my full-proof strategies of success to win over your prospects before your competitors do. Your competitors won't even see what hit them. They will be left so far back in the race that you will need to send signal flares to have them find their way back into the race or game.

Don't feel bad about this. You deserve it! It's time for *YOU TO WIN!* And, if you still feel bad about it, then you can send your competition a huge gift basket each month with all the newfound income and business you just acquired from them. Fair enough? Let's get started!

"IF YOU CHANGE THE WAY
YOU LOOK AT THINGS,
THE THINGS YOU LOOK AT CHANGE."
-WAYNE DYER

CHAPTER 1
TEN CITY DOMAIN

The very first thing we need to do to help knock out the competitor's edge is to build an advertising campaign that points to our company rather than theirs. The goal is to direct as much traffic to you and your company while at the same time taking the traffic away from your competition.

Here's the way it works. All you have to do is take your main domain name and search and secure the same name but add 10 different city's names to it. Those cities can be geographically around you if you would like. The point and goal is to start marketing yourself as the expert in other cities as well. But, you will simply forward all of those domain names over to your main domain and website. For example... If one of your main sites is www.MotivationKing.com (yes, I just made that up. No, I don't know if it's taken yet.) Anyway, let's say that's your site and let's say you primarily work in the Dallas, Texas area. Then, with The 10 City Domain technique, you would secure these other sites as well...

www.HoustonMotivationKing.com, www.StLouisMotivationKing.com www.KansasCityMotivationKing.com, and so on and so on. With most domains costing only about $12 a year nowadays, this will literally only cost you about $120 for the year to solidify all 10 of those city's domains. Then, you simply have to do some targeted online marketing in each of those cities. You will soon be taking your competitions bread and butter and placing it into your hands.

Another way you can use this technique, which is a little bit more direct and well, let's just say it... *harsh*! Here's what you do. Make a list of the top 10 competitors in your area or field. Take a look at each of their business names or website domain names. For each competitor, you simply creatively determine a strategically similar name and you secure that particular domain name. Make sure to remember to forward it to your main site.

An example would look like this. Let's say you have a competitor who has the site www.PoolMasters.com (I'm making this up. Not even sure if it's a real site or company). You could go ahead and solidify www.RealPoolMasters.com. See how this will work in your favor?

"Motivation is what gets you started. Habit is what keeps you going."
-Jim Rohn

CHAPTER 2
RAISE YOUR RATES!

One of the best techniques we incorporated within my companies across the board was to raise our rates on all of our products and services. At first, this sounds like it may affect our production in a negative way. But, I'm here to tell you that it did exactly the opposite... it boosted our revenue and production. It also did 3 other things that we were very pleasantly surprised at.

1) It moved our so-so clients who really saw the value in working with us, into long-lasting relationships and long-lasting followers.

2) It freed up a ton of time for our team in not having to deal with those 'iffy' clients who were sitting on the fence complaining a lot.

3) We started to see an increase of steady new clients moving from our competitors over to working with us on a long-term basis.

CLIENT LOYALTY IS KEY!

We believe we started to see the steady new client acquisition moving over from our competitors because of one major reason. Once they saw that we valued our products, service, and our time more than our competitors valued theirs, we believed these new clients decided that was a true value and trusted us more since we trusted ourselves and put our rates where our mouths were. There's a saying around my office that I instilled into all of my employees which goes like this: "The cheapest is typically the most expensive!"

The Pareto Principle, also referred to as the 80/20 Rule, is so vital here. Think about it, by raising your rates you will be weeding out those clients who are not really spending a lot of money or revenue with you, yet they seem to still take up the most amount of your time. You want to flip this around and start focusing on those clients (the top 20%) who are spending a great deal of revenue and money with you. These are the ones who should represent 80% of your revenue and income. By raising your rates, you are literally weeding out those 'low spenders' and quite frankly, the 'pain-in-the-butt' clients who are now free to waste your competitor's time and efforts.

"YOU CAN DEVELOP ANY HABIT
OR THOUGHT OR BEHAVIOR
THAT YOU CONSIDER
DESIRABLE OR NECESSARY."
-BRIAN TRACY

CHAPTER 3
OFFER OUTRAGEOUS
CONTESTS

We started to implement this idea years ago, and saw a bunch of clients jump over from our competitors to our side! Everyone loves to see what all the '**buzz**' is about. And, that's exactly what you want to do… create a huge buzz!

Think about it. When you hear of a huge contest going on … or you hear about something outrageous that's happening down the street, it's only natural to want to go check it out. So, that's what we started to do. We would set up a contest for those clients who bought a specific product or signed up for a specific service of ours in the next 7 days.

We would put them into a raffle to win a prize. The key is to make it a **GREAT** prize, like a new Harley Davidson motorcycle or a new Apple computer! The bigger, the better. And, ONLY for existing and new clients!

"REMEMBER THAT FAILURE IS AN EVENT, NOT A PERSON."
-ZIG ZIGLAR

CHAPTER 4
BUILD CHARITIES AROUND MEDIA

Everyone loves a charity! Everyone wants to give back. And, everyone loves it when they can combine their charity donations with their existing purchases that they need to make in the first place.

So, here's where you come in. What you want to do is become a matchmaker. Go to your local media outlets, such as radio, television, and print/newspapers. Set up an appointment with each of them and discuss which charities they are supporting. Then, let them know you would like to support them in their efforts and that you would love to promote them and their charities to all of your existing clients. They will be thrilled! Then you mention to them, as a 'by the way,' you would welcome any and all media exposure or article write-ups or exposes that they would like to do on you and your company to highlight this new collaboration between the two of you. Boom, free media exposure!

Special Charity Donations For Your Clients:

Wait, you're not done with this technique yet! Now, what you want to do is set up a special for your higher tiered clients. For those clients who are your A-listers and spend a certain amount of revenue per year with you and your company, you will make a donation in their name to a certain charity of your choice. Of course, you now make sure you are donating to one of your media affiliates. I know, brilliant! And, trust me, your competitors are not doing this at all. In fact, please keep this technique a secret!

"Companies that solely focus
on competition will die.
Those that focus on value creation
will thrive."
-Edward de Bono

CHAPTER 5
CUSTOMER SERVICE FIVE
GOLDEN RULES

There are 'Customer Golden Rules' that we instill in our teams within my companies. These rules are never to be broken. You should incorporate these as well and watch customers flock to you, rather than to your competition.

Customer Service

I. **The Customer is 'most of the time' always right!** You may be thinking this may be a typo. No, no typo. What we have found is that about 80% to 90% of the time, we will side on the customer's wishes. But, there's always a small percentage of customers who you simply need to hold your ground with and stick to your guns and your company policies in order to not allow certain customers to walk all over you. Sometimes, letting some of these customers go is actually a breath of fresh air and allows you to focus more on your customers who are there for the long run with you and build that long-term relationship.

2. **Customer Service is** everyone's **job within your company!** It's one of the biggest pet peeves we hear from clients. They say that they were simply not treated well when they called in. Or, one of the team members said that it wasn't their area to handle that particular issue. We suggest that you train every single one of your team members to take responsibility and ownership as if it were their company.

3. **Bonus Your Customers every time you connect with them!** Once we adopted this concept, we kept hearing that it was one of the main reasons why the customer picked our company to spend their hard earned money and time

with. Each time our customers call into our company with a question, we, of course, answer the question and find the solution... and then as an added bonus, we let them know we would like to give them a gift and send that over to them simply for reaching out to us. You can gift them an extra E-book you may have, or a special training video program that you have tucked away for a rainy day. The secret is for you to always have an extra gift in your back pocket for them. They will start to feel GREAT about calling you and leave the phone conversation feeling all warm and fuzzy inside. That's exactly what you are striving for. People tend to forget what you say or do, but they always remember the way you made them feel!

4. **Be a QUICK responder!** We have a rule to connect with the customer as soon as possible to acknowledge them and their concern. This means if they call in and leave a voicemail, you will respond back within a 1-hour period. If they send you an email, you respond back within a 3-hour period.

5. **Adopt a "YES" attitude and culture!** We decided to simply change our whole philosophy, attitude, and culture within our whole company to a "YES" one! This means that as often as we are humanly able to, we will give a "YES" answer to each and every customer. I'm not saying this is easy to do… but, well worth it in the long run once you adopt this into your corporation.

"Positive thinking will let you do everything better than negative thinking will."
– Zig Ziglar

CHAPTER 6
YOUR CUSTOMER IS FAMILY!

Once you come to the realization that your customers are literally paying your bills and making you super wealthy, you will start treating them like the super-rich Grandfather you wish you always had!

Your customers should always be treated like 'family!' I'm not talking about all of your customers. I'm talking about the customers who are your higher end clients. Once they reach a certain threshold as a client of yours, you should start inviting them to your house for personal mastermind sessions and retreats which you would only hold for your family members. Embrace them as a family member, and they will start treating you in kind. They will stick with you through thick and thin. Invite them to special occasions in which you will praise them for being in your life. This will absolutely piss off your competitors and leave them in the dust!

"Success is nothing more than a few simple disciplines, practiced every day."
-Jim Rohn

CHAPTER 7
THE REVERSE TESTIMONIAL

No one on the planet is doing this except for me! You know how and why I know this? It's because I made this technique up and have been guarding it as a secret for years! Well, here it is. I'm asking you to do me a favor. Please feel free to use the technique, but don't tell anyone about it. Keep it a guarded secret!

THE REVERSE TESTIMONIAL

Actually, it's quite simple. All you do is take your smartphone out and grab an assistant or a friend or colleague and ask them to record a video of you. Then, once they start recording, you simply give a great testimonial out to some-one you would like to highlight. It could be one of your clients. It could be your chiropractor. It could be your re-altor you just had help you sell one of your homes. I try to do at least one a week... so about 50 testimonial videos a year.

Part of the secret is that you are not going to tell the person what you are doing the testimonial for. It will be a sur-prise. Make sure in your video testimonial, you introduce yourself with first your name, title, company, etc.... then go into talking about the individual or team you are doing the testimonial for. What I like to do is say sometimes like ... "You know, there are three things that really stand out when I think about John Smith and what he's doing with the community. Number one, He really knows how to treat his clients as if they are family. Number two, he pays such attention to detail ... and number three, he is the most re-sult and solution oriented person our company has come across. These are the main reasons we trust John and use him and his team for all of our needs!"

Now, after you have completed your video testimonial for this person. Here's the BIG SECRET… instead of sending the video directly to him or her…. in fact, DON'T send it directly to them! What you do is something much better. You upload your video to your own **YouTube** channel and tag it under a playlist of "**People I Go-To!**" Then, you send him or her the actual YouTube link of the video you just recorded for them. It's brilliant! They will be so happy and surprised you did this for them, and they will want to share it with everyone… which in reality they are really sharing and promoting **YOU**, and not your competitors!

"A Clear Vision, Backed By Definite Plans, Gives You A Tremendous Feeling Of Confidence And Personal Power."
-Brian Tracy

Chapter 8
Give Informative Talks

Another cool way to piss your competitors off is by being known as the leading expert and leading source of knowledge in your industry. But, that's not all you have to do. You have to be a clear and present danger to your competition. One way to do this is to offer to give informative talks to assist the community. You want to give talks like these at places they will be at as well... such as Chamber functions and civic club meetings. Make sure you are finding the ones that your competition are members of.

Happy Hour Is On Us!

You can also set up monthly happy hours & invite your amazing clients to boast how awesome they are! Client appreciation goes a long way to solidify that your clients stay with you and not jump over to your competition. Oh, make sure to invite your competition as well. Even if they kindly say 'no thank you,' continue inviting them! TRUST ME ON THS ONE!

"PEOPLE OFTEN SAY MOTIVATION
DOESN'T LAST.
NEITHER DOES BATHING
--THAT'S WHY WE RECOMMEND IT DAILY."
-ZIG ZIGLAR

CHAPTER 9
CREATE A TOP 25 BOOK

To build a great audience of prospects and potential future customers, while at the same time ditching your competitors… you want to create and announce your company's Annual TOP 25 BOOK!

THE TOP 25 BOOK

This will be a book or magazine that you create and have published and printed in which you highlight 25 of the top 'alliance partners' you and your company are using that year. You could actually do this quarterly if you would like to. Other companies are going to beg to be in your book because they know it's prestigious and will give them a ton of exposure and marketing for their respective businesses … and it won't cost them a dime. This book will literally cost you pennies on the dollars of success for you and your company. Think about it. What if you could gain just one more client from one of your competitors on a monthly basis. Would that be worth it?

Rules of Engaging:

You want to make sure you include every single one of your team members in this project. What I mean is you need to make sure your whole team is talking about this prestigious book every single day and building the anticipation of who 'made the list'! This will build so much buzz and your competition will definitely hear about it. Furthermore, your competitor's clients will actually get mad at them for not having something similar. It's brilliant!

Include Your Media Alliances:

Don't forget to present a press release to your media alliances about your highly anticipated Top 25 Book due to be released on a certain day. Get the buzz going as much as you possibly can.

Include On-Going Sponsors:

You can also include and welcome some on-going sponsors to donate towards the cost of your project and books to offset those expenses, in exchange for including them as a sponsor in the back of your books.

"YOUR BIG OPPORTUNITY MAY BE RIGHT
WHERE YOU ARE NOW."
-NAPOLEON HILL

CHAPTER 10
BUILD A VALET SYSTEM

Cater to your existing clients as well as your brand new clients by setting up an awesome valet system! What I mean by this is pick them up! However possible, literally pick them up. Now, I obviously don't know what your industry is, but you need to find a creative way to pick your clients up and knock their socks off. If you have clients who come to meet you at your office, send a town car or limo to pick them up for the appointment. If you have clients who prefer to drive to meet you, set up a beautiful red-carpet concierge welcome for them. Do anything that is super awesome and creative to blow them away in a positive way. If you are meeting them for a luncheon meeting at a restaurant, and the restaurant doesn't actually have a car valet, then you should hire one of your assistants to stand in front of the restaurant waiting for them while you are inside at the table. Instruct the client to simply pull up to the front of the restaurant and let them know you have one of your 'Drivers' waiting for them to take care of their vehicle so that they can relax and not worry about parking at all.

"ABUNDANCE IS NOT SOMETHING
WE ACQUIRE.
IT IS SOMETHING WE TUNE INTO."
-WAYNE DYER

CHAPTER 11
BUILD A SOCIAL MEDIA ENVY

Your job here is to hire a professional who can make you and your company look like a superstar in your industry! Don't try to do it all yourself. Trust me on this one. Your time is better spent doing what you are great at. Leave the social media and marketing up to the experts.

That being said, it's imperative for you to have a great presence online in which your potential customers will pass over your competitors and find YOU first. This means you need to rank one of the top 10 in Google search engines. What does Google own… pretty much everything. So, your job is to use Google as much as you possibly can to build your business and crush the competitors. This alone will piss them off so much that you will start to get in their heads each day!

Create a Positive Culture

Stop, and I repeat... Stop posting things about your competitors, politics or religion! No one wants to see this except for those who are simply wasting their whole day online. This is not for you! Don't get me wrong, politics and religion are very important. But, the time and place for you to build your business is not by surrounding yourself in arguments online with people you don't even know, about subjects like those. So, just stop it!

Rather, build and create a positive culture on your pages on each of your social media platforms. It's up to you to teach others how you want to be treated on your own pages. Bring positive stories and awesome experiences that have a teaching curve to your posts. Education without boredom is key.

Be Yourself!

The worst thing you can do on Social Media is try to be someone you are not. So, be yourself... be authentic... be funny. People love that and will engage more with you on your pages. This is key to gathering more followers. Keep in mind, the only reason to gather followers is to convert them into clients in the future. Otherwise, you are simply hanging out for no reason and wasting valuable time.

Incorporate Facebook LIVE Posts

By now, I'm sure you have seen some Facebook Live posts. I know, I know, some of you are terrified of these and think there's no way you will ever do one. Well, haven't you ever been scared of trying something new, only to realize it wasn't that bad after you gave it a go? Same thing applies here. Give it a go! It's easy. Just click the 'live' button and be natural, be yourself, and have a conversation. That's it. Pretty simple. Beat your competitors to this and watch your business grow.

Just Do It

Like Nike says 'just do it,' you too should just DO IT! Vow and commit to yourself that your team will do at least 2 Live posts each week for the next 12 weeks. Once you start doing them, you'll get the hang of it. Include your clients in these posts as well.

Be Funny

People love funny. It's just part of nature. When you are authentically funny and not take things so seriously or up-tight, people tend to be attracted to that. They get enough negativity in their lives from other sources. Many people are watching these posts to simply get motivated.

Be Informative & Focused

Make sure you come into Social Media with a plan. It doesn't have to be all written out or anything… but at least have 1 or 2 main points that you will be covering in your

Live posts. Trust me, you will veer off on different subjects. But, that's okay as long as you have the main topics that you plan to discuss and refer back to them.

Describe Your Posts

Make sure you take the quick second to actually type in the tag line or subject line of your Live post. This will draw followers to come watch you and engage with you. (Secret Tip: Once you type in your description, double tap to copy it just in case you need to paste it in again due to poor reception areas.)

Welcome Your Clients

This is SO important! Make sure as people start to come onto your Live post... you are welcoming them to your broadcast or show. People love this. They absolutely love to hear their name and company name on the air. It makes them feel very special. I always welcome every single person when they come on to my shows. You can also highlight a few of them and compliment them on their businesses, etc.

Take Questions and Answers

Just like when people love hearing their own names called out, they also like it when you read their questions and answer them. This is where you can shine and make it super interactive. It takes on legs of its own and really starts to make you and your company look like a hero, expert, and authority in your industry.

Timing

Switch it up a bit. Some of your Live posts can be quick for like 2 to 3 minutes. Others can be 10 to 15 minutes long. Then, on occasion, you may want to go a little longer if you're really diving into a subject matter and including your clients in the conversation. Encourage this.

Location

It's also good to change up your locations on where you do your Live posts. People get bored easily. Changing up locations helps them stay interactive and wondering where you are. In fact, I suggest that you set it up to do a different Live broadcast at a different client's location or office each week. Highlight your clients and your competitors will start to realize you are crushing them and dominating that specific industry.

"Don't join an easy crowd;
you won't grow.
Go where the expectations and the
demands to perform are high."
-Jim Rohn

CHAPTER 12
BUILD YOUR WALL OF FAME

Testimonials are so vital to gaining the trust of your prospects and solidifying the sale. Studies tell us that one testimony from a credible source is worth about an hour of your presentation. Start building a wall of video testimonials from your happy clients and have them praise you for such an amazing and thorough job you did. The more detailed, the better.

Train your clients on how to give you a great testimonial. First of all, remind them that this is not only going to help you... but it will also help them because you would like them to introduce themselves first in the video by saying their full name, their title, their company name and a tag line that they typically use. It's free advertising for them! Then, they can go right into saying some great things about you and highlighting your amazingness.

Great Format of a Great Testimonial

"Hi guys, my name is John Smith. I'm the Regional Vice President of XYZ North America… where your business is our business! But, enough about me. Today, I want to talk to you about Erik Swanson. Wow, he came in and did such an amazing job with our whole distribution team here in the United States, where not only did he have the whole sales team fired up, but he had all of the Branch and Logistics Managers high fiving him after the meeting! After searching a lot of other choices, I'm positive he was the right choice for our regional meeting, and we are now looking at bringing him in to speak and train at our national conference at the end of the year. If you're looking for a great speaker who comes from the heart, look no further. Hire

Erik "Mr. Awesome" Swanson! You will absolutely thank me!"

Now, that's a great testimonial. Simply ask your client to introduce themselves for about 15 or 20 seconds, and then say some great things about YOU for the next 30 to 45 seconds. Ask them to mention they are glad to pick YOU over your competitors. That will turn into a fantastic video testimonial that you can add to your 'Testimonial Playlist' on your YouTube Channel and start giving that link out to people.

"YOUR LIFE ONLY GETS BETTER
WHEN YOU GET BETTER."
-BRIAN TRACY

CHAPTER 13
HIRE THE COMPETITION

Okay, even I think this one is a tiny bit sneaky. But, what the heck… here's what you do: You hire your competitor's old employees or team members. Who better to have a grasp on what your competition is doing or planning to do than someone who used to work there. I'm not saying to do anything too crazy or sneaky. But, there's nothing wrong with bringing on to your team someone who has inside intelligence from some of the companies you are trying to crush and dominate. If you are able to hire them, this means that they did not have what's called a 'NCC,' or a 'Non-Compete Clause.'

Note, though, that you indeed want to have a 'NCC' with this new hire or any new hires for that matter. You simply don't want to make the same mistake your competitor did by allowing a rep or employee work for you and then go to another company in the same industry with any trade or company secrets of yours.

"Learn how to be happy with what
you have while you pursue
all that you want."
-Jim Rohn

Applied Knowledge is
power.

BONUS #1 INTERVIEW THE COMPETITION

This technique is once again kind of on the sneaky side. So, close the book now if you don't want to find out what this one is about. But, it's a good one!

Here's what you do. You send one of your newer team members to your competition to inquire and request information as if they were interested in hiring them. Don't allow your competitor to know that this team member works for you. That's a very important part of this strategy. Make sure your team member asks many questions to find out as much as they possibly can about what they are offering, including discounts, terms, refund policies, etc., etc. It is said that knowledge is power, which is only half true. Actually, applied knowledge is power. Learn as much about your competition as you can.

"THINK CONTINUALLY ABOUT
WHAT YOU WANT,
NOT ABOUT THE THINGS YOU FEAR."
-BRIAN TRACY

BONUS #2 THANK YOU CARDS IN ADVANCE

Take a moment each week to send 'Thank You' cards to your potential new clients and prospects in advance! Yeah, that's right, in advance. It's amazing when you receive in the mail an awesome card or thank you note saying something like this…

I wanted to THANK YOU in advance for connecting with me and allowing me to buy you lunch one day. I would love to sit down and see how we can assist each other with our businesses and referral generation. Please let me know when a good time for you would be. I travel a ton with our companies and ventures, but I'm happy to change my schedule around to connect with you!

I guarantee you that you will get the meeting and appointment and completely blow your competition away with this one!

"IF YOU GO LOOKING FOR A FRIEND,
YOU'RE GOING TO FIND THEY'RE SCARCE.
IF YOU GO OUT TO BE A FRIEND,
YOU'LL FIND THEM EVERYWHERE."
-ZIG ZIGLAR

BONUS #3 THE $100 GIFT CARD!

Stop, and I repeat, STOP giving out stupid $10, or $15 or even $25 gift cards to gas stations or even coffee places. It's cheesy and makes you look like a cheapskate! Trust me on this one. Here's what you should do. Invest in yourself by investing in others! Go down to your nearest Starbucks or your favorite coffee place… or an awesome steak place that's well known. Grab five $100 gift cards. Hold on to them until you meet those contacts who you really want to connect with and build a business with. A few days after you met them, go ahead and send them one of my "Thank you cards in advance" and include a $100 gift card…. and this is the important part… add to the thank you card something like this: "Looking forward to connecting and helping each other with our businesses. In fact, lunch is on me (Or coffee)!". Trust me, they will have to spend the card on YOU! You literally get your $100 back and get the client at the same time!

"IF YOU CANNOT DO GREAT THINGS,
DO SMALL THINGS IN A GREAT WAY."
-NAPOLEON HILL

BONUS #4 MORE FREE MEDIA

Would you like even more free media? The answer, by the way, should always be 'YES'! Okay, here's another way you can do it. Use "HARO" which stands for "Help A Reporter Out." This service started back in 2008 by our friend Peter Shankman. He originally started it as a Facebook page, which has quickly turned into an amazing source for you to get your expertise out to the world! The website is www .HelpAReporter.com. If you are looking for the media to find you and highlight you and your company, then this is the place to go to. In fact, media outlets such as Fox News, The N.Y. Times, The Wall Street Journal, Chicago Tribune, and even Time Magazine, among many others,use HARO to find stories of success and make it a lot easier for their journalists. It's an absolute win-win. Use it now and keep it a big secret from your competition.

"HOW PEOPLE TREAT YOU IS THEIR KARMA;
HOW YOU REACT IS YOURS."
-WAYNE DYER

BONUS #5 TARGET FOCUS

Continue to 'Target Focus,' rather than focus on your competition. One of the biggest mistakes I see businesses, as well as entrepreneurs, make is that they bombard their own mindsets and ultimately their attitudes with thinking about their competition. Just stop it! Just as Wayne Gretzky did in his sport of Hockey, he focused on the puck and where it was going, rather than focusing solely on the opposite team. The more you focus on you, your business, and your clients, then more success you will have. It's inevitable. Use the 'law of attraction' rather than the 'law of distraction.' You must laser focus on your outcome and target and leave everything else to your competitors to deal with. Don't allow yourself to stoop so low as to get caught up in that drama. Your team members will thank you for having such a positive, target focused attitude and direction.

"Expect the best.
Prepare for the worst.
Capitalize on what comes."
-Zig Ziglar

CRUSH & DOMINATE HOMEWORK

CRUSHING & DOMINATE STYLE!

Now it's time for you to embrace these steps and take action on at least five of the strategies in this book in the next seven days! The only way you will grow and succeed is by taking action. Pick your favorite five techniques and implement those right away. Then, strive to implement another five techniques the next week… and so on. We love to hear amazing stories of triumph and conquering, and we welcome you to join our secret society of 'Crush & Dominators'! Email your success stories.

stories@CrushandDominate.com

"Patience, persistence,
and perspiration
make an unbeatable
combination for success."
-Napoleon Hill

CONCLUSION

GROW BY CRUSHING & DOMINATING!

We live in a society where we will always have people trying to get ahead of us. It's time for you to get ahead of all of them! Enough is enough! To grow, you must crush and dominate. It's just like going to the gym to work out. In order for your mussels to grow, you literally must tear them down. This is the only way they will grow bigger and stronger. It's the same way in business. I know you want to be nice and get along with everyone you come across. And, that is fine to do with your prospects, customers, and long-term clients. But, it's about time we draw that line in the sand when it comes to your competitors. It's called 'Shark Tank' for a reason.

We love to hear amazing stories of triumph and conquering. And welcome you to join our secret society of 'Crush & Dominators'! Email us your stories and who knows, we may include you in our Top 25 Book in the future.

stories@CrushandDominate.com

"WHEN YOU DANCE, YOUR PURPOSE
IS NOT TO GET TO A CERTAIN PLACE
ON THE FLOOR.
IT'S TO ENJOY EACH STEP
ALONG THE WAY."
-WAYNE DYER

CRUSH & DOMINATE

VIDEO TRAINING SERIES

It's imperative to harness all of these techniques and it may take a little bit more than simply reading about each technique in a book like this. This is why we have assembled a complete video training series program for our "CRUSH AND DOMINATE"! You will learn the tried and true secrets which catapulted so many business owner's, entrepreneur's, and sales professional's success. Eliminate your competitors now and see a clear path for you and your company to grow as one of the TOP in your field. You deserve it! Don't delay. Let's get started right away. Erik "Mr. Awesome" Swanson is here to help you.

Grab a discount by using Promo Code: DOMINATENOW

www.CrushandDominate.com

"Erik Swanson has such a unique way of teaching the steps to success. Even if you believe you're at the top of your game already, Erik will help you raise the bar even higher!"

- Ruben Gonzalez ~ Four Time Olympian, Speaker, Author

"A GOAL IS A DREAM WITH A DEADLINE."
-NAPOLEON HILL

SOCIAL MILLIONS PROGRAM

JOIN THE PROGRAM!

We have assembled an amazing video program for you to learn the steps to build your social media, marketing, and branding awareness as well as social exposure! Our program takes you step-by-step in building what you will need to succeed in business these days and gain the followers and the steps to convert those followers.

Allow Mr. Swanson to personally teach you exactly what he used to build such an International Platform of followers. In fact, he has also set up a JV (Joint Venture) for those who want to take advantage of it and promote the Social

Millions Program to their list of followers as well. He feels you should be compensated nicely for your efforts. We have done *ALL* of the work for you. All you have to do is sign up, learn, and refer people you care about to check out the program. It will sell by itself. You will earn a commission for each person you refer to our program. It's our way of saying Thank You! Simply go to:

www.SocialMillionsProgram.com

"YOU CANNOT BE LONELY IF YOU LIKE
THE PERSON YOU'RE ALONE WITH."
-WAYNE DYER

Speaker Erik Swanson

Book Speaker Erik Swanson for your next event!

30 to 45 Minute Keynote Speech $5000.00

60 Minute Keynote Speech/Workshop $7500.00

60 to 90 Minute Speech and Training $9000.00

1/2 Day Training System (3 hours) $12,500.00

Full Day Training System (5 hours) $20,000.00

Team@CrushandDominate.com

www.CrushandDominate.com

Meet Erik "MR. AWESOME" Swanson. Erik Swanson has delivered over 6300 motivational presentations at conferences and meetings worldwide. As an award winning International Keynote Speaker, Best-Selling Author & Attitude Coach, Erik Swanson is in great demand! Speaking on average to more than one million people per year, he is both versatile in his approach and effective in a wide array of training topics. Respectively nicknamed "MR. AWESOME" by many who know him well, Erik invites some of the most talented and most famous speakers of the world to join him on his coveted stages, such as Brian Tracy, Nasa's Performance Coach Dr. Denis Waitley, Co-Authors of the book & movie 'The Secret,' Bob Proctor, Jack Canfield, John Assaraf, The Millionaire Maker, Loral Langemeier, and Co-Author of 'Rich Dad Poor Dad,' Sharon Lechter, among others. Mr. Swanson has created and developed the super popular Habitude Warrior Conference which boasts a

2-year waiting list and includes over 33 top leaders around the world in a 'Ted Talk' style event. It has quickly climbed to one of the top 10 events not to miss in the United States! www.SpeakerErik.com

Made in the USA
San Bernardino, CA
28 August 2017